BEACH EXPLORER

50 THINGS TO SEE & DISCOVER

HEATHER BUTTIVANT

Illustrations by Grace Helmer
Designed by Emily Sear

Printed in Poland on paper from responsibly managed, sustainable sources by Hussar Books

ISBN 9781912836734

September Publishing
www.septemberpublishing.org

BEACH EXPLORER

50 THINGS TO SEE & DISCOVER

HEATHER BUTTIVANT

CONTENTS

INTRODUCTION

Whether the beach you visit is a picture-perfect paradise, a rocky rubble or a muddy mess, it is full of secrets and mysteries. It is a gateway between our world and the deep oceans, a place that is changing before our eyes. If you know where to look, the shore is home to some of the strangest creatures on our planet.

This book is packed with **easy activities** and **brain-busting facts** that turn any beach trip into an adventure. Use your detective skills to find out how beaches are made, investigate wildlife families and reveal some incredible survival secrets. You will then uncover the threats facing our marine wildlife before completing your final challenge.

Prepare to answer questions that have puzzled people throughout the world, such as:

- Where does sand come from?

- How do starfish scrub their backs?

- How long does it take a 'biodegradable' balloon to break down in seawater?

- And, most important of all, how can you make sure the seagulls don't snatch your ice cream?

Now it's over to you! Pick **activities** that appeal to you and suit the beach you are visiting. Discover more about each topic in the **fact files** and try out a tremendously tricky **quiz** at the end of each chapter. You will soon be on your way to becoming a top **beach explorer!**

If you're planning to explore a beach, be sure to go prepared.

BEACH RULES

 Don't get caught out by the tide. Put your location into a tide times website or check a local tides booklet. Start exploring well before low tide and make sure your way off the beach is clear.

 Dress for the weather. Always wear wellies or beach shoes to protect your feet. Don't forget a hat, sun protection and a water bottle in hot weather.

 Follow signs. Many beaches have signs telling you about dangers. Stay away from cliffs, unstable rocks and surging waves.

 Look after the wildlife. Move slowly and carefully. If you want to look closely at a sea creature, keep it in a bucket of seawater for a few minutes before returning it. Avoid disturbing birds or marine mammals.

 Leave nothing behind except your footprints. Litter is bad for marine wildlife so take everything home with you.

 Beaches are fun but they can be dangerous. Go with an adult and make sure someone knows where you are. If you see someone in serious trouble or find yourself in danger, get help by calling the coastguard on **999**.

CHAPTER 1

BEACH DISCOVERY

Your first challenge is to unlock the mysteries of how your beach was made and how it is changing over time.

These explorations will take you on a journey through millions of years of history. Along the way, you will encounter the incredible forces that move rocks and oceans and meet animals and plants that endure some of the most extreme conditions on Earth. You'll also uncover evidence of how your beach is still changing today.

Like all great explorers, you will need to open all your senses and be prepared for some surprises!

Sand Detective

ACTIVITY
1

Where does sand come from and why does it feel comfortable to walk on? Your first activity is to become a Sand Detective!

Study the **cliffs** from a distance and explore the **rocks, shells** and **pebbles** on your beach.

- Look at the colours of the rocks and shells. Are they similar to the colour of the sand?

- Does the sand contain mud or very tiny grains? If so, can you spot a river or stream nearby?

- Is the sand the same size and colour in every part of your beach?

- Can you figure out what the sand is made of?

What's Happening?

The sand on your beach starts out as larger rocks and shells which often come from the cliffs and seas close to the beach. Over a long period of time, these have been broken down by the power of the waves. Rocks and mud can also be carried to the beach from far inland by rivers.

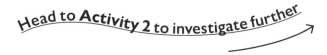

Head to Activity 2 to investigate further

Sand Under the Magnifying Glass

You may have noticed that the grains of sand on your beach are different **colours**. What else can you find out? It's time to get up-close.

- Put some sand onto black paper. This will help the colours stand out.

- Use a magnifying glass, hand lens or a microscope to look at your sand.

- What do you notice about the size of the sand grains? Can you see tiny shells in your mix?

- Are they smooth and rounded or jagged and rough?

What's Happening?

You will probably find lots of transparent crystals of a mineral called quartz in the sand. Quartz is very hard and does not dissolve in water. While softer rocks erode or wash away, quartz is left behind. Marine biologists can examine sand to identify what species of seashells are living near the beach.

Dig Deeper

Dark-coloured sand sometimes contains magnetite, a mineral that can be used to make iron. Try dragging a magnet through the sand. Any magnetite will stick to it.

Q **Fact File: Sand** × +

Waves and wind are constantly attacking the rocks around the coast. The sea pushes the rocks and dead seashells around, breaking them down into smaller and smaller pieces. Eventually this makes sand.

Sheltered beaches with small waves tend to have coarse sand. Some have only large pebbles, known as **shingle**. At exposed beaches with large waves, the sea pounds the sand into tiny, well-rounded pieces to create fine sand.

When waves reach the beach, they slow down and drop their load. This builds up into a beach. The sea can also wash sand away. Rivers carry mud and rocks to the shore. As they near the sea, rivers widen and slow down, so they drop the sediment they are carrying. This makes some beaches muddy, providing food for all sorts of animals.

Fact File: Sand

Why So Tense?

When sand is wet, it has water trapped in the pores between the grains. The water has **surface tension**, which is the same thing that allows some pond insects to walk on water. This helps to hold the grains together so that you can make sandcastles from it.

Musical Sand!

When grains of sand are small enough and the amount of moisture is just right, the layers make a whistling or singing noise when you walk on them. There are over 30 beaches in the British Isles that claim to have singing sand.

One, Two, Three . . .

There are tens of thousands of grains in just one teaspoon of sand. Mathematicians have estimated that the total amount of sand on all the world's beaches is around 5,000 billion billion grains.

Strange Sand

In some places sand is made mainly of coral, gemstones or even from the skeletons of tiny animals called foraminifera.

ACTIVITY 3

Find the High Tide Line

If you have ever spent time on a beach, you have probably noticed that the edge of the sea isn't always in the same place. At **high tide** there may be no beach left to walk on, while at **low tide** there can be kilometres of golden sand.

Stand at the top of your beach and look for a line of stranded seaweed and debris, often stretching all the way across the beach. This is called the **high tide line** or **strandline**.

- What has been washed up?

- Is there more than one line on your beach? Why might this be?

- Where is the highest point that you can find things dropped by the sea?

Dig Deeper

To get an idea of the power of the tides, try filling an empty bucket with seawater. It's pretty heavy. Now think about how many buckets of water are moved up and down your beach twice each day by the tide.

Tide Fort Champion

ACTIVITY 4

Pick a calm day with small waves and an incoming tide. Find a clear patch of sand below the tide line, a few metres away from the edge of the waves. Grab a spade and see if you can stop the sea!

Dig a trench at the front of your fort and pile the sand up to make a wall. Continue the walls to make sides and a back, making your fort as tall as possible.

- How long does the tide take to reach your fort?

- How does the sand change its appearance after the waves hit your walls?

- Challenge your friends and family to a fort-building competition.

Stay safe as the tide comes in. You will have to abandon your fort eventually!

Dig Deeper

- Look at the high tide line on different days. How much does it move?

- What do you think the beach would be like if there were no tides?

Q Fact File: Tides × +

Gravity does useful things like stopping us flying off into space when we jump. The bigger and denser an object is, the more gravity it has.

Tides are caused by the **gravitational pull** of the sun and moon. This pull creates two bulges in the ocean on opposite sides of the Earth. As our planet spins, the bulges travel across the oceans and we see them on the beach as the tide coming in.

The moon has the biggest pull on our tides because it is close. The sun is much larger but it is a long way away. When the sun and the moon line up, the tide comes in further and goes out further. This is known as a **spring tide**. When they are not lined up, we have smaller **neap tides**.

When the tide is high, the level of the sea goes up, like filling a bath. The difference between the highest and lowest level of the sea is called the **tidal range**.

Q Fact File: Tides ✕ +

The Tide Line

The incoming tide pushes debris like seaweed, shells and rubbish with it. The tide line marks the highest point the sea has reached that day. You may also find older tide lines from spring tides or storms higher up the beach.

Tidal Waves?

Tsunamis are sometimes called 'tidal waves', but they are caused by earthquakes under the sea, not tides. Tsunami waves can be up to 10 metres tall and can travel at 800 kilometres per hour.

Tide Power

Tides are a form of **renewable energy**. This type of energy source doesn't run out. We can use tides to create electricity by passing the water through a turbine, but tidal power schemes can cause problems for marine wildlife, shipping and fishing.

Disappearing Roads

At low tide you can use a causeway to walk or drive to some islands, like St Michael's Mount in Cornwall, Coney Island in Ireland and Cramond Island in Scotland.

Make Your Own Salt

If you play in the waves or go swimming in the sea, it won't be long before you taste the **salt**. On hot sunny days, the rocks on the beach heat up quickly and are perfect for this experiment.

- Pour a tiny amount of seawater from a rock pool onto a hot rock. Wait for the sun to evaporate away the water, leaving the rock dry.

- Look closely. Can you see white crystals glistening? If so, congratulations! You have made some salt.

- Use a magnifying glass or hand lens. Can you see what shape the salt crystals are?

What's Happening?

You cannot see the salt in the water because it has **dissolved**. This means that the salt crystals have completely broken up and mixed with the water molecules. When water heats up, it turns to steam and evaporates. As the water **evaporates** the salt crystals are left behind.

Explore Life in the Briny Sea

ACTIVITY 6

How is wildlife affected by salt? Let's explore the beach to find out.

- Find some pools on the beach. Small pools at the top of the beach will lose water through evaporation, especially on sunny or dry, windy days. These pools will be saltier than normal seawater.

- Find a small pool that is especially salty and compare it to a larger one. Do these pools have the same plants and animals in them?

- Now compare them to pools closer to the sea and spot the differences.

What's Happening?

Very salty pools have just a few types of plant and animal living in them. Not many living things can survive in very salty environments. You are likely to find the biggest variety of animals and seaweeds living in pools further down the beach where the salt levels are kept steady by the sea.

Dig Deeper

How do you think tides, rainwater, winds and the seasons might affect the amount of salt in the pools?

Q Fact File: Salt × +

Seawater contains many different salts, but most of the salt is the same type we use in our food: **sodium chloride**.

The salts in the sea come from **rocks**. When rain falls on land, it dissolves small amounts of salts and other minerals from the rocks. **Rivers** carry the salts to the sea. Salt is also made by underwater hot springs called **hydrothermal vents**. In the sea, these salts build up to make the water salty.

Marine wildlife uses up some salt. Most marine plants and animals need just the right amount to survive. Too much or too little would kill them. Luckily, the amount of salt in the sea stays about the same. This is because some salt is absorbed into the sediment on the ocean floor and eventually turns back to rock.

Q Fact File: Salt ✕ +

No Swimming Lessons Required

Mixing salt into water makes it denser, which helps things to float better. The Dead Sea in southwestern Asia is actually a huge lake and it's so salty that you can't sink in it.

Fancy a Cup of Seawater?

If you're stranded at sea, don't be tempted to drink the water. The salt will make you pee more and make you dehydrated. Drinking pee is a better option, but that could make you ill, and would also taste disgusting!

Secret Seas

Rock salt, formed when an ancient sea dried out 200–300 million years ago, can be found under parts of Cheshire, Northern Ireland and Yorkshire.

A Dash of Salt?

Around 3.5% of the weight of seawater is salt. That might not seem much, but one cubic kilometre of seawater on average contains around 23 million tonnes of salt.

Love Your Limpets

Limpets are sea snails. They can be found on rocks and man-made structures like sea walls and quays. Their yellow-brown shells are cone shaped, like a paper hat.

As the tide goes out, locate some limpets.

- Sometimes you can see one twist as though it's dancing on the spot. What might it be doing?

- Look around the rocks for circular grooves. Can you see how they're made?

- Put an ear close to the limpets. Can you hear a grating, crackling sound?

- Gently push against a limpet's shell. Do you feel it shift? If you touch it lightly again, does it feel easier or harder to move?

What's Happening?

Limpets live on rocks that are exposed to all the elements. To survive, they grind their shells against the rock to create a groove. By pushing their shells into this groove and gripping the rock with their powerful sucker foot, limpets protect themselves from the dry air. Limpets feed on seaweed by scraping with a saw-like organ. This chips off pieces of rock, which makes a crackling noise.

Press Seaweed

Plants on the beach are full of surprises. Below the tide line, you enter the realm of seaweed. These plants have no roots or flowers, but are as beautiful as any garden plants.

Pressing seaweed is a lovely way to appreciate the different colours and shapes of the weeds. You need a deep tray, a sheet of heavy paper (watercolour paper is ideal), greaseproof baking paper, paper towels, newspaper and heavy books.

- Rinse your seaweed in fresh water.

- Part fill your tray with water and place your sheet of watercolour paper at the bottom.

- Float your seaweed over the paper until you are happy with the position. Slowly lift the paper out.

- Gently dry with paper towels and lay on some newspaper. Cover with a paper towel and some more newspaper.

- Place between heavy books. Check each day and change the newspaper and paper towel until your pressed seaweed is completely dry.

- Admire your dried seaweed!

Q Fact File: Life at the Extreme ✕ +

Life on the beach is tough. It can be baking hot or freezing cold. Wildlife that lives near the top of the beach has to endure being plunged underwater and dried out by the wind over and over again. Few flowering plants and grasses can survive these conditions. They only grow above the tide line and tend to have tough, thick leaves to keep the water in. They may also have red leaves when they are struggling with too much salt.

Below the tide line, only seaweed and seagrass can grow. Seagrasses are flowering grasses that can make meadows underwater. Seaweeds are **algae**, which grow in water and don't mind the salt.

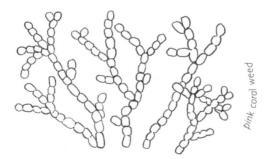

pink coral weed

Q Fact File: Life at the Extreme ✕ +

Seaweed Ice Cream?

Most seaweeds are edible. Laver seaweed is used to make laverbread in Wales. Carrageenan, which comes from seaweed, is sometimes used as a thickener in ice cream! In Japan some red seaweeds are called nori and are used for wrapping sushi.

Boy or Girl?

All limpets are male when they are young. As they grow older and bigger, they become female.

Grass Glue

Marram grass has long tangled roots, around a metre long, that help hold sand dunes in place. It is being used in parts of China to try to hold back the Gobi Desert.

Spot Signs of a Changing Beach

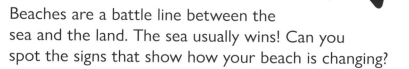

Beaches are a battle line between the sea and the land. The sea usually wins! Can you spot the signs that show how your beach is changing?

Tick off any signs you spot:

- ☐ Caves or rock arches
- ☐ Rock falls
- ☐ Rocks and islands in the sea
- ☐ Streams or rivers
- ☐ Different layers of rock or sediment visible in the cliffs
- ☐ A layer of rounded pebbles in the cliffs
- ☐ Man-made sea walls or piles of rock
- ☐ Groynes (Fences or walls running from the top to the bottom of the beach)

What's Happening?

There are many clues to how your beach may have once looked, and what caused the changes. In the distant past, the rocks you see may have been in layers of sediment formed under a tropical ocean. A layer of pebbles in the cliff could be an ancient **raised beach**. Waves wear down rocks. Rivers, estuaries and currents carry sediment, bringing vital supplies to build the beach up. Over thousands of years, these small events make a big difference.

Hunt For Fossils

Fossils are ancient animals and plants that have been naturally preserved. They are often millions of years old and lived at a time when your beach was a very different place.

- Search for fossils among any loose sedimentary rocks and boulders lying on the beach. Stay away from cliffs and landslips.

- Fossils often look like drawings on the rocks, but are sometimes three-dimensional.

- Try to identify and label your finds. Look up when they lived and what the climate was like. Do they have living relatives?

bivalve fossil

Rock Types

Sedimentary: Made of sand or mud built up in layers then compressed. Most likely to contain fossils. Sandstone, shale and limestone are sedimentary rocks.

Igneous: Made of cooled magma or lava. Very rarely contain fossils. Basalt and granite are igneous rocks.

Metamorphic: Started as another rock type but changed through heat and pressure deep under the Earth's surface. This normally destroys fossils. Slate and marble are metamorphic rocks.

Q Fact File: Changing Beaches

The **continents** on Earth move very slowly over time. Many of the fossils on our beaches were formed under the sea millions of years ago, a time when Britain lay south of the **Equator** and had a hot, tropical climate. Imagine how great the summer holidays would have been if humans had been alive then!

Much faster changes take place on beaches. Cliffs are eroded by the waves and wind, storms change the sand level and dunes grow and shrink. By understanding these changes, we can start to predict how beaches might change in the future. For example, we know that the soft clay cliffs of the Holderness Coast in Yorkshire shrink back by up to ten metres per year.

ammonite

Fact File: Changing Beaches

Why Are Some Cliffs White?

Long ago, when much of Britain and Europe was under the sea, the skeletons of tiny algae called coccoliths came together on the seabed. Over time, the weight of the sediment turned them into a rock called chalk which formed the white cliffs.

Lost Creatures

Ammonites had spiral shells and were related to squid and octopus. There are more than 10,000 species of ammonite in the world's fossils, but there are none alive today.

Fossil Fetch!

A 197-million-year-old Ichthyosaur skeleton discovered on a Somerset beach in 2019 was named 'Poppy' after the dog that found it! Ichthyosaurs were marine reptiles that looked similar to dolphins.

Lava Legend

The Giant's Causeway in County Antrim, Northern Ireland, is made of hexagonal pillars of cooled lava. Local legend says that the causeway was built by the warrior Fionn mac Cumhaill so that he could cross the sea to pick a fight with a Scottish giant.

How Do Worms Change the Beach?

There are some surprisingly **tiny creatures** that can shape the shore. These animals mostly live on beaches with mud or soft rocks. If you feel that you are sinking into the mud at any time, stay safe and stay away.

Walk down the shore looking for **casts**. These are curly piles of sand and are found next to round pits about the size of a small coin. The curly sand is lugworm poo. The pit is near the lugworm's head.

- Carefully, dig down between the worm cast and the pit from one side with a spade or trowel.

- What do you notice about the burrow?

- If you would like to look at the worm, pop it in a bucket of seawater. Put the worm back and fill in your hole. Watch out: lugworms can bite!

What's Happening?

Muddy sand can be pongy because **bacteria** that live there let off gases that smell of rotten eggs. Lugworms draw seawater into their burrows from the surface. The **oxygen** in the water creates a whole new habitat for other life, and gives the burrow a paler colour than the surrounding sand.

Find Evidence of Sponges and Piddocks

ACTIVITY 12

When people want to dig mines, they use serious machines, yet some small and squidgy sea creatures make tunnelling into solid rock look, well... boring!

- Look for rocks or shells riddled with tiny holes. Can you guess what makes them?

- Go further down the beach and search for deep holes about the width of a pencil in large rocks. If you look down the holes you might see movement.

- Why might holes be more common in some types of rock and shell than others?

What's Happening?

If shells or pebbles have lots of tiny holes, it is usually a sign that they have been attacked by a **boring sponge** using chemicals. Sponges are easy to recognise as they feel spongy!

boring sponge

Larger holes are made by a clam shell called a **piddock**. Piddocks twist their shells against the rocks to create a burrow where they are safe from predators. These creatures are helping to break up the rocks and speed up erosion.

Fact File: Animals that Shape the Beach

When we look at the building blocks of a beach, it is important not to forget the wildlife. These creatures may be tiny and seem completely powerless compared to the tides and waves, but some build new environments while others destroy rocks and other structures. All these forces working together are what makes each beach unique.

Ghostly Glow

Piddocks aren't just amazing rock borers, they actually glow in the dark! They make mucus that gives off a blue-green light.

Beehives on the Beach?

Even though each honeycomb worm is only around 3–4 cm long, by working together these industrious animals can build structures up to a metre high. They look like huge honeycombs made of sand.

Q Fact File: Animals that Shape the Beach × +

That Sinking Feeling!

Christopher Columbus is known as the European colonialist who accidentally landed in the Americas. On his fourth voyage, in 1502, shipworms put holes in his boats. He had to spend over a year in Jamaica before he was rescued.

Go Gribbles!

Gribbles are woodlouse-like marine animals. They produce chemicals called enzymes in their digestive juices that can break down wood. These enzymes could be used to turn waste into an environmentally friendly liquid fuel for our cars.

Bacteria Cities

Stromatolites are towers of very tiny organisms called cyanobacteria, thought to be one of Earth's first lifeforms. Living stromatolites can still be found today, such as those at Shark Bay in Australia.

Beach Discovery Quiz

Have a go at these quirky questions or test your parents and friends!

1 What colour is the sand at Mahana Beach in Hawaii?

☐ a) Blue

☐ b) Red

☐ c) Green

☐ d) Black

2 The world's biggest tidal range occurs in the Bay of Fundy. Where is that?

☐ a) Canada

☐ b) South Africa

☐ c) Greece

☐ d) Chile

3 Which of these fish can only survive in salt water?

☐ a) Common eel

☐ b) Cod

☐ c) Sea trout

☐ d) Salmon

4 What did Storm Ciara uncover on an Isle of Wight beach in 2020?

a) A 3,000-year-old picnic

b) An ancient forest

c) Atlantis

d) A fossil dinosaur footprint

5 How are gribbles causing problems in New York?

a) Chewing away at supports beneath Brooklyn Bridge Park

b) Gnawing at the foundations of the Statue of Liberty

c) Climbing the Empire State Building

d) Shortening Long Island

How did you do?
Turn upside down to find the answers.

Answers: 1: c - The beach is made out of olivine crystals from a volcanic eruption 49,000 years ago. 2: a - The Bay of Fundy has a maximum tidal range of around 16 metres. 3: b - The others live in both seawater and freshwater during their lifecycle. 4: d - The 130-million-year-old clay footprint probably belonged to either a *Neovenator* or a *Spinosaurus*. 5: a - Brooklyn Bridge Park is built on wooden supports and the gribbles have moved in for a picnic.

CHAPTER 2

WILDLIFE FAMILIES

Strange things happen at sea, so people say, and there are few things stranger than sea creatures.

Your second mission is to meet some of the residents at your beach and find out about the families these animals belong to.

From flower-like **anemones** to five-armed **starfish**, be prepared to meet life which is not quite as you know it. Discover amazing adaptations to underwater life, watch animals in action and find out about their weird and surprising abilities.

Make Your Own Plankton Net

Plankton is the name for living things that float in the sea and are carried by currents. Arm yourself with a pair of tights to catch plankton and find out about our first wildlife family: the crustaceans. You may need an adult to help you.

Step 1
Bend a piece of wire into a circle. Use tape to fasten the ends together.

Step 2
Using scissors, cut off one leg from an old pair of strong tights. Fold the open end of your tights over the wire circle. Sew it in place using a needle and strong thread.

Step 3
Take an empty plastic bottle and cut off the bottom (keep the lid on). Cut a small hole in the toe of the tights. Fit the tights over the cut end of the plastic bottle. Secure with string and tape.

Step 4
Tie three 50 cm pieces of string at equal intervals around your wire hoop. Tie the loose ends onto a key ring. Tie a longer piece of string to the key ring.

Drag your plankton net through a pool or shallow water. If you are successful, your bottle will contain a milky concentration of plankton that might include baby crabs.

Be Kind to a Crab

ACTIVITY 14

Crabs are in a family of animals called crustaceans. **Crustaceans** have more than four pairs of legs and breathe through **gills**. They don't have bones on the inside like us, they have a shell on the outside instead.

Grab a bucket and prepare for a close encounter with a crab!

- Search areas with damp rocks and seaweed. Always put everything back as it was.

- To pick up a crab, first place a finger on the centre of its shell and press down lightly. Use the thumb and index finger of your other hand to hold the sides of the shell under the 'armpits' of the crab's pincers.

- On your crab's underside you will see a line making a triangle shape. This is its tail.

- Male crabs have a narrow triangle. Female crabs have a wide-based triangle.

Dig Deeper

Put one crab in a bucket of seawater. How does it move? Remember to put it back afterwards.

Q Fact File: Plankton and Crustaceans   ✕   +

Most plankton are tiny. They can be squidgy, spiny, armoured, bug-eyed, colourful, transparent or even glow-in-the-dark. A single teaspoon of seawater can contain millions of individual plankton, including viruses, bacteria, animals (**zooplankton**) and plants (**phytoplankton**).

Crustaceans are a big group of animals that include crabs, lobsters, prawns, hermit crabs, barnacles, sand hoppers and woodlouse-like animals called isopods. Releasing their babies into the plankton is a clever survival strategy. Young crustaceans can drift a long way and easily populate new places.

World's Longest Animal?

Siphonophores are chains formed of lots of individual plankton animals. An *Apolemia* siphonophore found in deep water off Australia was 45 metres long.

Take a Deep Breath

Phytoplankton make their own sugars to eat by taking in sunlight and carbon dioxide and giving out oxygen. They are responsible for producing between 50% and 85% of the oxygen that we breathe.

Fact File: Plankton and Crustaceans

Closer to Home. . .

Woodlice are crustaceans. They live on land but they breathe through gills. Some crustaceans also live in rivers and ponds.

Creepy Crustaceans

Some crustaceans are gruesome **parasites**, attaching themselves to fish and sucking their blood. Some wily barnacles enter the bloodstream of crabs and take over their brains and bodies!

What's Under a Crab's Tail?

Female crabs keep their eggs under their tails. When the baby crabs are ready to hatch, their mother stands on her back legs and jiggles her tail to release them.

Night Light

Sea sparkle plankton produces light (a process called **bioluminescence**) when it is disturbed. It can make breaking waves glow in the dark.

Shell Collecting

Picking up pretty shells is great fun! Have you ever wondered why their colours and shapes vary so much? What might the animals that live inside look like? It's time to check out this marvellous **mollusc** family.

Walk along the tide line filling a bucket with all the empty shells you can see.

- Draw a triangle in the sand big enough for all of your shells.

- Go through your shells and put all the ones that are the same in piles together.

- Place the most common shells in the base of your triangle, the next most common above and so on.

cockle

- Why do you think there are more of some types of shell than others?

What's Happening?

The most common shells on your beach will belong to molluscs that can find plenty to eat. These are usually snails like limpets that feed on seaweeds, or clams like cockles that filter plankton out of muddy water. The shells at the top of your triangle may be carnivores!

painted top shell

Secret Trapdoors, a Snail Investigation

Explore any rock pools near the top of your beach. It shouldn't take you long to find a live sea snail to observe.

- Carefully lift your snail off the rock. Can you feel it sticking?

- Put your snail in a pool or bucket of seawater and wait for it to poke its head out.

- If you are patient, you may see its tentacles and 'tail'.

- Gently pick your snail up and turn it over to watch it return into its shell.

- Can you see how it seals itself into its shell? Why do you think it does this?

What's Happening?

Sea snails die if they dry out, so at low tide they are in great danger. Their secret weapon is a kind of trapdoor, called an **operculum**. Sea snails retreat into their shells and pull their trapdoors shut behind them. They also make mucus that dries and sticks them to the rock.

Dig Deeper

Use a guide to identify your shells. How many different species can you find?

Q Fact File: Molluscs

Many molluscs have hard shells to keep themselves safe from hungry hunters. They all look different because they are cleverly adapted to living in different parts of the sea and eating different foods. Some molluscs look very much like land snails while others, like mussels, razor clams and scallops, have shells split into two halves. These are called **bivalves**.

Molluscs have squidgy bodies and a muscular foot which they use to crawl or swim. There are around 85,000 known species of mollusc in the world today and most of them live in the sea.

Sea snails, clams and sea slugs come in many bright colours and surprising shapes to help them hide among seaweeds, sea squirts and sponges. Cuttlefish, squid and octopus are also molluscs and belong to a group called the **cephalopods**, meaning 'head-feet'. They have evolved to swim and catch prey and have amazing eyesight.

Q Fact File: Molluscs ✕ +

Violet Assassin

The violet sea snail has devised a clever way to hunt down its prey. It creates a raft of mucus bubbles (like snot bubbles) and floats upside down on the surface of the sea. It travels alongside other ocean drifters, feasting on them.

Half Plant, Half Slug?

Most sea slugs are carnivores, but the solar-powered slug is a super-vegan. It chomps on seaweeds then keeps the part of the plant that produces sugars, the chloroplasts, inside its body. The chloroplasts carry on reacting to sunlight, making extra food for the slug.

Super Spies?

Octopuses would make great secret agents. They can change colour, unscrew jam jars, fit their boneless bodies through tiny gaps and squirt ink at attackers. Most only have mild venom, but the blue-ringed octopus can paralyse a human in 10 minutes!

Boy or Girl?

Many molluscs aren't just boys or girls: they are both at the same time!

How Do Starfish Scrub Their Backs?

Everyone loves a starfish! They are an instantly recognisable rock pool creature. They are not related to fish at all but are part of an animal family called the **echinoderms**.

If your beach has rock pools, there's a good chance there are some starfish hiding there. For this activity you will need a magnifying glass. Remember that if you move anything in your search for a starfish, you should put it back as you found it.

- Look under shady overhangs and under loose stones for a starfish with thick, stiff arms.

- Pop your starfish in shallow water or in a bucket.

- Look closely at its back. What can you see?

What's Happening?

A starfish's arms cannot easily reach its back. So, the starfish's back is covered in tiny pincer-like structures. It uses these little pincers, called **pedicellariae**, to pluck off any pesky pests.

What Makes Starfish Arms Special?

The starfish you are most likely to find is called a **cushion star**. It is a pale, orangey-brown colour with a puffy centre and short arms. It is usually just a few centimetres across.

- Find as many starfish as you can.

- Look at the arms of each starfish. Are they all the same length?

- Do all the starfish have five arms? Do you think they can survive with fewer arms?

If your starfish has any arms that are shorter than the rest, it is busy re-growing them! Sometimes starfish get carried away and grow extra arms, just because they can.

Dig Deeper

- Turn your starfish upside down in the water. Can you see the starfish's tube feet?

- Starfish have simple eyespots in the ends of their arms but they cannot see like us. What other information might your starfish use to decide where to go?

Q Fact File: Starfish × +

Starfish, urchins and sea cucumbers are all members of the echinoderm family. This means they have spiny skins. These spines help to protect the animals from predators. They are a fascinating family with some strange and gruesome habits.

urchin

Disgusting Dinners

When a starfish finds something it wants to eat, it pushes its whole stomach out. It uses its digestive juices to turn its prey to soup, then sucks its stomach back in again. Yum!

No One Got the Brains in this Family!

Starfish and their relatives have no brain. They feel things and respond using a simple nerve ring.

Q Fact File: Starfish × +

Getting to the Bottom of a Sea Cucumber's Defences

Cotton spinner sea cucumbers can squirt a cloud of sticky white threads out of their bottoms to entangle or confuse attackers.

Heartless Echinoderms

Echinoderms have no heart or blood. They take oxygen in through special plates in their skin and use water to move gases to their tube feet.

No Arm, No Problem!

A starfish can lose an arm and just carry on. In fact, sometimes they lose three or four arms. It might slow them down for a while, but they soon recover!

Ninja Limpets

Starfish like nothing better than to munch on molluscs, but the common limpet fights back. It lifts one side of its thick shell and slams it down, slicing through the starfish's tube feet.

Tentacles Experiment

Anemones are jelly-like animals that look rather like colourful flowers, with long tentacles in place of petals. They are members of a huge group of sea creatures called the cnidarians. For this activity you will need to find an anemone in a rock pool with its tentacles open.

- Use a small piece of seaweed or an object like a pencil.

- Gently touch it against the ends of the anemone's tentacles.

- Very slowly, pull your object away.

- What happens?

If you touch an anemone with your fingers, wash your hands well in warm water before you touch your eyes.

What's Happening?

Many marine animals make themselves comfy on a rock and wait for the currents to bring food to them. It's like having a take-away brought straight to your waiting mouth! The animals in the cnidarian family, including anemones, catch their prey using stinging cells called nematocysts. When anything brushes against their tentacles, these cells shoot little barbs like harpoons and inject a toxin. This is why the tentacles seem to stick to your seaweed.

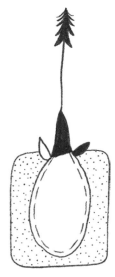

nematocyst cell

Anemones in Action

Anemones will never win many prizes at sports day, but are they moving?

- Find a comfortable spot to watch an anemone that has its tentacles open.

- Are the tentacles only moving with the current?

- Try gently touching your anemone with seaweed again. What do the tentacles do?

What's Happening?

When they sense food, the anemone's **tentacles** become active. They curl inwards to stop any thieving crabs or prawns making off with their snack. Anemones are not fast walkers, but they can squidge a short distance along the rocks or let go and drift to a new spot. If anemones get too close to each other, they may hit each other with their tentacles.

Dig Deeper

- Find an anemone that is out of the water. Where are its tentacles now? Why do you think anemones need to hide their tentacles?

- Jellyfish are also cnidarians. If jellyfish are washed up on your beach, look at the colours on the top to identify the species. Be very careful not to touch as some have a nasty sting.

Q Fact File: Anemones and Jellyfish

Cnidarians have stinging cells and usually have a symmetrical body with a central mouth. From corals to jellyfish, the cnidarians are a fascinating and sometimes terrifying group of animals. They are present in oceans all around the world.

Small but Deadly!

The Irukandji box jellyfish is only around 1 cm in diameter but has the most powerful sting of all jellyfish. It doesn't live in European waters.

Jumping Anemones!

Some anemones can swim to find a better spot or escape predators. They aren't great swimmers so they have to bounce along the seabed like a pogo stick!

anemone

Fact File: Anemones and Jellyfish

All For One and One For All!

Some cnidarians like the Portuguese man o'war are colonies, made up of lots of individual animals. Each one has a job to do and they work together to survive.

Safe Among the Stingers

Clownfish live among the tentacles of tropical anemones. In European waters, the Leach's spider crab does the same thing, hiding in the green tentacles of snakelocks anemones.

Meant to be Together

Some corals and anemones keep microscopic algae inside their tentacles. The anemone protects the micro-algae and the micro-algae make sugars for the anemone to eat.

Climate Crisis

When corals are under stress due to changes in temperature, light or food, they often lose the micro-algae that live inside them. When this happens they turn white and may die. This is called **coral bleaching**.

Find a Fish, Design a Fish

Fish come in a bewildering range of colours, shapes and sizes. **Flatfish** are a great example! They start life as normal-looking fish, then turn flat with a spotty top side and eyes on top of their head. This might look weird, but it is the perfect design for hiding on a sandy seabed. Let's investigate what makes a **successful fish** on your beach.

- Search for a fish in a pool. Look at its colour and how it moves.

- Think about what might help a fish to survive in this pool. What colours will help it to blend in? How can it stop predators eating it? How will it find food?

- Use your ideas to design a whole new fish species. Draw your fish on paper or in the sand and give it a name.

What's Happening?

Lying on their sides in the sand must have helped the flatfish's ancestors to hide from their prey and their predators. Over many generations the fish became flat! This process is called **natural selection**.

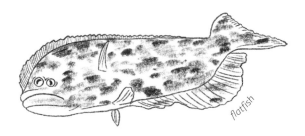

flatfish

How Fish See Without Being Seen

Many fish swim in the **open water** and need to **hide** in plain sight. How do they do it? Try this activity to find out how.

- Collect some dark and light pebbles and place them in a transparent bucket or jar filled with water.

- Place your bucket on a dark surface. Looking from above which colours are easiest to spot?

- Hold your bucket up and look from underneath. Which colours stand out now?

What's Happening?

Many fish are white underneath and darker on top. This makes it harder for sea birds to notice them against the dark ocean. Their colouring can trick predators that are looking for darker shadows underneath their prey. Fish often have silvery scales which work together with their skin to reflect light, making them difficult to spot from above.

Dig Deeper

- What other animals use this trick to help them to hide from predators and prey?

- Search for information about fish that live around your beach and their shapes, colours and behaviours.

Q Fact File: Fish   × +

Fish are extremely varied, but all fish have **gills**, live in the water, and none of them have fingers or toes. Most have a backbone and fins to swim with and most are **cold blooded**. This means their temperature changes with the temperature of the water around them.

Magic Slime!

Hagfish are strange looking creatures with no proper backbone. When they feel stressed, they give off weird slime that expands to 10,000 times its original size. A teaspoon of hagfish slime can fill a big bucket!

Fish Out of Water

Blennies, also known as 'shannies' or 'sea frogs', are common rock pool fish. They can survive out of water in holes in the rock for many hours by breathing through their skins.

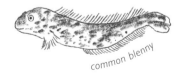
common blenny

Q Fact File: Fish ✕ +

Bendy Bones?

Some fish, like sharks and rays, have skeletons made of cartilage. It's softer, more bendy and lighter than bone. If you want to feel what cartilage is like, squidge the end of your nose.

Pregnant Fathers

Female seahorses and pipefish lay their eggs into the male's pouch or belly-groove. He looks after the eggs and gives birth to the babies!

Cuddle a Catshark?

Catshark skin is so rough that in the past, it was used by fishermen as sandpaper.

Transforming Fish

Wrasse are colourful fish that start life as females but can decide to become male as they grow older.

Twenty-Minute Bird Count Challenge

ACTIVITY 21

There are lots of different species of birds that live around our coasts. For this activity, a bird identification guide will be handy and a pair of binoculars if you have them.

herring gull

- Set a timer for twenty minutes.

- Count how many different types of bird you can spot.

- What do their beaks look like? Look at the length, thickness, shape and colour.

- How do you think each bird might use its beak?

- Look up the birds you spotted to find out their names and more about their lives.

What's Happening?

Each bird has developed a beak that is the best tool for its job. **Turnstones** have short, sturdy beaks for flipping over pebbles and gobbling up bugs. **Oystercatchers'** beaks are long and sharp to smash open shells. **Cormorants** have spear-like beaks for fishing, while **sandpipers** have thin beaks for worm digging.

puffin

oystercatcher

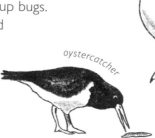

60

Operation Save Your Sandwich!

Circling above the beach, perched on the pier or pacing on the sand, beady-eyed herring gulls are on the prowl. They know exactly what they want and how to get it. . . and what they want is your lunch!

By observing these master chip-chompers, you'll learn how to avoid their attention and discover that they're pretty amazing birds.

- Find a spot with a good view of a crowded seafront where people are eating.

- Look out for herring gulls, which have silver-grey wings and a yellow beak with an orange spot. Young herring gulls are a mottled brown colour.

- Watch where the gulls fly and stand.

- How does their behaviour change if they spot people eating?

- Look out for raids on food. Where do the gulls approach from?

- Can you work out the best ways to avoid losing your lunch to a herring gull?

Dig Deeper

Herring gulls might seem common, but their numbers are going down. What do you think can be done to help them find food, build their nests and stay safe?

Q Fact File: Seabirds   ×   +

Seabirds have to be tough to survive storms and find food. Herring gulls are successful because they eat lots of different foods and even **scavenge** dead creatures. Human food isn't healthy for them though. They can also get into trouble by eating plastic wrappers and landing on roads. You can help seabirds by never feeding them and taking litter home with you. Eat with your back against a wall and cover your food with your hand to avoid surprise attacks.

Who Needs Helmets?

Gannets dive headfirst to catch fish, hitting the water at 95 kilometres per hour. They have pockets of air in their neck and shoulders which they use like airbags to reduce the shock.

Puking Petrels!

Fulmar petrels can open their beaks and spit out vomit at high speed, covering any would-be attackers in stinky oil.

Fact File: Seabirds

Disposable Disco Beaks?

Puffins are known for their big colourful beaks. Scientists have recently discovered that puffin beaks are fluorescent, glowing blue under ultraviolet light. The colourful part falls off in winter, leaving a simple grey beak.

White a Lot of Poo!

Nesting seabirds poo a lot, so much that they often turn the cliffs white. In the past, seabird poo was big business. It was collected as a fertiliser called guano to help plants. This trade was bad for seabirds as people disturbed their nesting sites.

Fantastic Flight Path

Arctic terns have the longest migration of any bird in the world, flying up to 35,000 kilometres per year. They spend their summers in northern countries, including the UK and Ireland, before heading all the way south to islands near the Antarctic during our winter.

Going Round in Circles!

Most eggs roll if they are put on a flat surface, but to stop their eggs becoming omelettes, cliff-nesting birds have eggs with a pointy end, shaped like a cone. This stops the eggs from rolling away.

Wildlife Families Quiz

Bamboozle your brain or test your teacher with these tricky questions.

1 How much does the largest fish species in British waters weigh?

a) Up to 6 kilograms

b) Up to 60 kilograms

c) Up to 600 kilograms

d) Up to 6 tonnes

2 When a barnacle swimming in the plankton is ready to settle down does it…

a) Work with others to build a house.

b) Cement its head to a rock.

c) Put on a pair of slippers.

d) Do a special dance with its feathery legs.

3 What happens to the great grey sea slug if it eats an anemone?

a) It eats just a few tentacles before the anemone stings it to death and gobbles it up.

b) It swells up and explodes.

c) It changes colour and is then able to sting anything that touches it.

d) It behaves as though it is drunk and cannot move in a straight line.

4 The UK is home to the world's smallest sea bird. What is it called?

a) Storm petrel

b) Puffin

c) Little grebe

d) Little Mix

5 Pearlfish can be found in tropical waters. Where do they sometimes make their home?

a) In the old shells of sea urchins

b) Inside divers' boots

c) Under a crab's tail

d) In a sea cucumber's bottom

How did you do?
Turn upside down to find the answers.

Answers: 1: d - The basking shark is the second largest fish in the world, measuring up to 12 metres, but don't worry, it only eats plankton. 2: b - Baby barnacles swim in the plankton but as adults they spend their whole lives with their head attached to the rock, waving their legs to catch food. 3: c - This slug keeps the colour and the stinging cells from the anemone in its body. 4: a - The storm petrel is not much larger than a sparrow and weighs up to 30 grams. That's less than a packet of crisps. 5: d - The less said about this one the better!

CHAPTER 3

SEASHORE SURVIVAL

Now that you have met some of the animals that live on your beach, it is time to uncover their secrets. Sly survival tricks and menacing weapons make the difference between life and death on the shore.

Life is tough in the **rock pools**. There's the danger of drying out at low tide or suffocating when the sun warms up the water. As if that wasn't enough to contend with, there are also seabirds hunting for snacks and other **heavily armed creatures** at every turn. Discover a world of cunning defences and awful table manners as you try out these activities.

If your beach doesn't have rock pools, you can still hunt for **mermaids' purses** and other eggs.

Create a Miniature Rock Pool

ACTIVITY 25

When you look into a rock pool, it may seem like there's nothing there! Some serious scientific experimentation will soon put that right.

To find out why the creatures can be hard to see, you will need two large pots or buckets; one white and one dark.

Step 1
Fill your white pot with seawater.

Step 2
Gently scoop up a few crabs, prawns and snails, etc. Go slowly and search underneath seaweed and stones to find creatures.

Step 3
Put your creatures in the white pot and watch them for a while.

Step 4
Next, put the animals in the dark pot. Does it make a difference to how easily you can see the animals?

Step 5
Finally, line either pot with sand, pebbles and seaweed to create a realistic rock pool.

Step 6
Pop your creatures in and watch closely. Can you still see them? Where do they go? Look out for changes in colour.

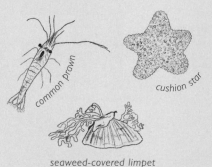

common prawn

cushion star

seaweed-covered limpet

Best-Dressed Animal Competition

ACTIVITY 26

This is the moment that your beach has been waiting for: a fashion show! Many animals spend their whole lives working on their splendid costumes. You may even struggle to notice the animal underneath the incredible outfit, so look closely!

- Explore the rocks and the pools, and look for limpets, mussels and crabs that have other living things attached to their shells. Popular decorations this season include seaweeds, barnacles, tubeworms and sponges!

- How many can you find? Who will win the prize for the best-dressed animal on your beach?

- Take photos of the best disguises and ask your friends and family to vote for their favourites.

- Why do you think animals let other creatures make a home on their backs?

Dig Deeper

- Use a magnifying glass to look closely at a prawn. You may see changing spots of colour.

- Play 'spot the creature'. See how many different animals you can count in one minute.

Q Fact File: Animal Disguises × +

Colour changes, sneaky hiding places and odd outfits make marine creatures masters of disguise! Being able to disappear helps animals to avoid being seen by **predators** that want to eat them.

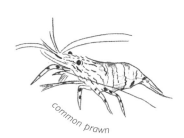

common prawn

Rock pool animals are easier to see against a white background than a dark one because they are adapted to hiding in dark pools. Many prawns are partly **transparent** so you can see right through them, and some prawns and fish can change colour. Brightly coloured snails soon disappear among the red, green and brown seaweeds. Being invisible to other animals is also a big advantage to predators that want to ambush their prey. Some animals take things to extremes!

Nothing to Seaweed Here!

Pipefish are long, thin brown fish. If any potential attackers come near, they stay completely still and pretend to be seaweed.

Q Fact File: Animal Disguises ✕ +

Decorated Velcro

Many species of spider crab have little hooks on their shells that work like Velcro. They attach seaweed and other living things to their shells so that they look like a seaweed-covered rock. Some spider crabs are covered in living sponges so you cannot see their shell at all.

See-Through Secrets.

Baby eels (known as elvers or glass eels), are completely transparent. This makes it hard for hungry predators to spot them. Their backbone is visible as a faint dark line and you can see their internal organs and their eyes.

Invisibility Cloak

Cuttlefish have taken the art of camouflage to near perfection. They can change both the colour and texture of their skin to exactly match their background, making them nearly impossible to spot.

Sandy Bottoms!

Lots of fish, shrimps and prawns are the same colour as the sand they live on. They like to burrow into the sand, making their disguises even more effective. Look for little jets of sand shooting up from the bottom of pools!

Egg Hunt

ACTIVITY 27

You can find eggs in the rock pools at any time in the **spring** or **summer**. Take a look and see what you find! Make sure you leave any eggs egg-xactly where you find them.

- Jelly patches on brown seaweed belong to snails like periwinkles.

- Yellow or purple capsules found under shady rock overhangs belong to a snail called the dog whelk.

- If you find any crabs, check under their tails for spongy egg masses.

- You might find groups of fish eggs laid under rocks.

- Spiral-shaped eggs belong to sea slugs. Tangled strings like pink spaghetti belong to a slug called the sea hare.

- Balls of green snot-like jelly on the seaweed are worm eggs.

How many types of egg can you find on your beach? Are the parents looking after the eggs?

What's Happening?

Some baby sea creatures hatch straight onto their food and start munching and growing. Crabs and prawns keep their eggs on their bodies until they hatch, while some fish guard their eggs.

The Protective Fish Father Challenge

Fish often guard their eggs, and this is usually the job of the dad. If you are lucky enough to find fish eggs, try using a **magnifying glass**. Can you see the **eyes** of the developing babies?

Don't worry if you haven't found any fish eggs. Have a go at being a daddy fish!

- Find a pool with plenty of creatures in it like prawns, snails and crabs.

- Put something new in the pool and pretend it is your precious clutch of eggs. Something edible is ideal, but a rock or shell will do.

- Sit quietly by your pool and watch. Every time anything comes near your object, shoo it away with a piece of seaweed.

- Imagine what it would be like trying to protect hundreds of tiny eggs, twenty-four hours a day!

Dig Deeper

Look out for worm pipefish on your beach. They have long, very thin brown bodies. Check the fish's belly to see if it is a male carrying eggs. Pipefish are related to seahorses.

Q Fact File: Sea Creature Parents

It's fair to say that most rock pool parents don't make much effort to care for their children. As soon as they're done laying the eggs, they squirm, skitter or slime away to find something to eat. **Hatchlings** in the plankton can be carried far away by currents and may never meet their parents. All that is needed to keep their species going is for some of the babies to survive.

Enormous Eggs!

Most sea slugs lay coils of eggs that are at least as big as their own body and often much bigger! The *Favorinus branchialis* slug likes nothing better than eating the eggs of other slugs.

Nesting Fish

Male wrasse don't only guard their eggs, they create nests for them out of seaweed which they gather in their mouths.

seaweed

Fact File: Sea Creature Parents

Moonlight Romance

Tropical corals cannot move about to find a mate. But when the moon, sun and temperature are just right, they all blast out their eggs and sperm at the same time. This gives these two ingredients the best possible chance to find each other and make baby corals.

Pregnant Fathers

Seahorse males keep their mate's eggs in their pouch until they have hatched and then puff out around 1,000 live babies all at once.

Egg-ceptional Fish

The ocean sunfish releases around 3 million eggs in a single season, more than any other known vertebrate.

A Rock Pool Weapon Inventory

Danger lurks around every corner in the rock pools. On this battlefield, the animals all have weapons and defences. Watch out for teeth, spines, poisons, acids and ink explosions as you investigate!

Find a mid-shore pool with plenty of creatures. Your challenge is to spot as many different types of animal as possible and work out what they use to defend themselves or attack others.

- What animals use claws? Do any have more than one pair?

- How many types of animal use hard shells? Do any have spines?

- Are there any fish in your pool? What might they use to catch prey?

- Can you spot any animals with stings, such as anemones?

- Are there soft animals? What might they use to put off would-be attackers?

What's Happening?

Even the most defenceless-looking animals have to survive. Many soft creatures taste bad or make nasty chemicals like acids to put off predators. Others have hard shells and sturdy claws to fight off enemies that come close.

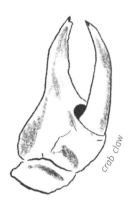

crab claw

Spy on a Hermit Crab Battle

Follow in the footsteps of great conservationists by watching how animals behave in the wild and discover their **secrets**.

If you spot a seashell sprouting legs and running away, it has a **hermit crab** inside.

- Find a pool with lots of hermit crabs in it.

- Spend around 10 minutes watching everything they do.

- How do they use their claws?

- What happens when something disturbs them?

- Are any hermit crabs fighting? What happens?

- Pick up a hermit crab by its shell and take a look at its claws. Are they both the same size?

Dig Deeper

Can you create your own marine creature battle cards game? Cut out around 20 cards and draw an animal on each. Add scores out of 100 for things like the creature's size, speed, camouflage, defences and weapons. Work out your rules and challenge a friend to play.

Q Fact File: Weapons

Sea creatures have enough weaponry to make the army green with envy. In the rock pools and in the wider seas beyond, unseen battles are constantly raging.

Although they like to live close to each other, hermit crabs often fight over shells and food. Most hermit crabs have one large claw for guarding their shell entrance and crushing food; the other smaller claw helps them eat.

Need a Nutcracker?

Large crabs can easily crush a walnut. The claws of coconut crabs, which live in the Pacific and Indian Oceans, are almost as powerful as the bite of a lion with a force around 90 times their own bodyweight.

Fact File: Weapons

Smoke Screen

The sea hare is a large sea slug that feeds on seaweeds. It might look like a blob of jelly, but if anything tries to attack it, it shoots out a cloud of purple ink.

Chemical Weapon

The yellow-plumed sea slug squirts out sulphuric acid when it is threatened. This chemical can melt skin and shells: it's definitely not something you'd want in your mouth.

In the Eye!

Sea squirts are simple blobby creatures which look like lunch to other animals. They don't have claws or teeth. When anything comes too close, they squirt a jet of water out like a mini water cannon.

Fishy Tasers

Some fish store energy from their muscle contractions and use it to zap their attackers or prey with electricity. Electric rays are found in the seas off the British Isles. They can deliver an electric shock powerful enough to knock a human off their feet.

Be a Super-Sleuth: Murder Holes

Have you ever wanted to be a **detective**? This is your chance to uncover the identity of a **dastardly murderer** who is operating along rocky shores. Examine the victims, search for clues and unmask the killer.

- Search for dead sea snails and clam shells on your beach. Gather as many as you can in a bucket.

- Go through your shells. Do any of them have a neat round hole in them? If so, you have found one of our killer's victims.

- What sorts of shell is the killer targeting most on your beach? Are all the 'murder holes' a similar size and shape?

- Is there anything left of the victim except its shell?

What's Happening?

The only murder weapon that could have done this job is a sea snail's radula. Some creatures like limpets use their saw-like radula to scour tiny seaweeds off the rocks, but not our suspect! Our mystery snail uses its **radula** to drill through the shells of other molluscs.

Be a Super-Sleuth: Line Up the Suspects

ACTIVITY 32

We now know that our killer is a sea snail. Can you catch it in action?

- Look at the underside of the snail shells you have found.

- Our killer hides its radula in a groove that sticks out of the opening of its shell. Do any of your shells have a tear-shaped opening with a groove?

- Search for living colonies of limpets and mussels. Is the killer's shell among them?

- You may spot the suspect sitting on top of another shell. If so, you have caught the murderer red-handed!

Our Gruesome Killer is the Dog Whelk!

This innocent looking snail softens the shell of another mollusc with chemicals and drills a hole with its radula. Using its stomach juices, it turns its victim to gloop. The dog whelk sucks up its meal using its radula like a drinking straw. Slurp!

Dig Deeper

On sandy beaches, look out for clam shells with neat holes. These killings may be the work of another common assassin, the necklace shell.

Fact File: Assassins on the Beach

Terrible table manners are common on the shore. Animals surviving in extreme conditions can't afford to be polite. Birds smash or grab their prey, crabs crush, fish bite, jellyfish and anemones sting and starfish dissolve their victims in disgusting ways. The dog whelk is successful because it is great at finding food and has a very hard shell that most predators can't crack open.

Dog Whelks in the Doghouse!

Mussels attach themselves to rocks with byssus threads. If a dog whelk tries to attack them, they shoot out their threads like lassos. The trapped dog whelk either dries out or starves to death.

dog whelk

Q Fact File: Assassins on the Beach ✕ +

Vultures of the Shore

Not all of the whelk family are killers. Netted dog whelks prefer to clean up crime scenes, eating the leftovers when animals die on the shore

Killer Babies

Dog whelk egg capsules can contain hundreds of eggs, but only a few survive. The first babies that hatch out usually gobble up the rest!

Meat Feast

Dog whelks aren't the only carnivorous snails. Cowries eat sea squirts, wentletraps feed on sea anemones and the common whelk is fond of worms and snails.

The Emperor's New Clothes?

A clothes dye made with a chemical produced by the dog whelk was highly prized in Roman times, especially to make ceremonial robes. The dye starts out as a clear liquid, but changes colour in sunlight, becoming green, then blue and finally purple.

Set Up a Fish Table

Sea creatures are often beautiful, but many are **messy** and **gruesome** eaters. So, who eats who and how? We're not done with disgusting dining yet . . .

For this activity you'll need food that sea creatures find tasty and that is safe for them to eat, such as a small piece of meat or fish. If you prefer not to use meats, try a bit of salad. Some rock pool animals will eat anything!

- Place your bait on a flat piece of rock in a pool with plenty of wildlife.

- Move back so that you are not casting a shadow and watch quietly.

- You may have to wait a few minutes before the animals become adventurous.

What's Happening?

If you are lucky, your bait will set off a feeding frenzy. Look out for fish like gobies that like to crocodile-roll as they attack, messy crabs that send pieces of food flying, and prawns that rush in to clean up the mess.

flat periwinkles eating seaweed

Find a Sea Creature's Bottom

Digestion is a simple process: we eat and drink, the food is broken down in our **stomachs** and **intestines**, and we **pee** and **poo** out the waste. As you'll see in this activity, some sea creatures don't follow the normal rules.

- Find a starfish, crab or anemone.

- Locate the animal's mouth (tip – turn starfish upside down).

- Now, find the animal's bottom.

Having trouble? Many rock pool animals only have **one opening** into their bodies. In these animals, their **mouths** are also their **bottoms**. Some anemones also spit their babies out of the same hole.

Crabs do have a bottom, but it is hidden by their shell at the end of their tail. Crabs also pee out of their faces! They have small holes at the base of their antennae for this purpose.

Dig Deeper

Watch your rock pool to see if you can discover what each animal eats. Can you draw the food chain from the top predator to the seaweed?

Q Fact File: Dinner and Digestion ✕ +

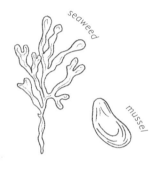

seaweed

mussel

Rock pool creatures may have some brutal and messy eating habits but they know how to survive. In the rock pools, seaweeds, plankton and detritus are at the bottom of the food chain. They are eaten by many types of worm, snail and small crustaceans which are, in turn, eaten by crabs, fish and seabirds. Although sea creatures have some strange ways of pooing, nothing goes to waste in the ocean.

World's Largest Poo

The blue whale, the world's largest animal, poos out enormous clouds of bright-orange rancid-smelling poo. It would be horrible to swim in, but this poo-cloud provides food for millions of plankton. These tiny organisms absorb carbon from the atmosphere and provide oxygen for us to breathe.

Fact File: Dinner and Digestion

Say Cheese!

Some fish have an impressive smile, complete with a full set of teeth. The common blenny (also known as shanny) is a common rock pool fish whose little white teeth are perfect for biting the legs off barnacles.

Bottomless Slugs

Sea slugs in the Calma family eat fish eggs. Their digestive system is so efficient that they produce no waste so they don't need a bottom and never poo.

Pooing Champions

Some species of flatworm are able to poo from holes all over their backs while others don't poo at all.

Carnivorous Seaweed

The food chain doesn't always work the way you expect. Normally animals eat plants, but one microscopic seaweed, *Karlodinium armiger*, is known to gang up and overpower small animals in the plankton.

Hunt for Mermaids' Purses

Mermaids' purses certainly look like they might hold treasures – the **two horns** at either end could be mistaken for an opening mechanism – but they are actually a **shark's** or **skate's** egg capsule. Can you find one?

- Walk along the high tide line.

- Look among the washed-up seaweed for shiny black, brown or green capsules with horns or curly tendrils at either end.

- Collect any you find and keep them for the next activity.

What's Happening?

Mermaids' purses are a sure sign that sharks or their relatives are living close by. They can be found at any time of year. Egg cases washed up on the beach are nearly always empty because the baby has hatched out successfully.

Greenish egg cases with curly tendrils at each end are laid by **catsharks**. Egg cases with two horns at each end are laid by **skates** and are darker brown or black.

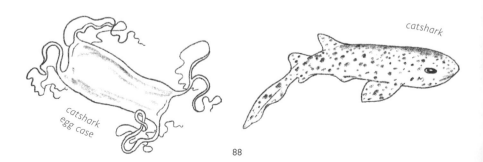

catshark

catshark egg case

Identify Your Egg Case

Now you have found an egg case, you probably have more questions. How big is the **adult**? What does it eat? How long does it take the baby to hatch?

- If possible, take your egg case home and soak it in tap water for a couple of hours.

- Remove your egg case from the water and grab a ruler to measure it.

- Find an identification key online – The Shark Trust have lots of resources.

- Go through each step to find out what species laid your egg case.

Dig Deeper

- How much can you find out about the species that laid your egg case?

- Make egg case hunts a regular activity when you visit a beach and record your findings to help shark and ray conservation.

- If you find a live egg case washed up on the beach, put it in seawater and contact a local aquarium. If it is attached to seaweed in a pool, leave it be.

Q Fact File: Top Predators

There are around 40 species of **shark** and 18 species of **skate** and **ray** found in British waters. There are probably some sharks living close to your beach. But don't be fooled by scary films! There are **no records** of unprovoked shark bites in British waters. **Top predators**, like sharks, are a vital part of the food chain. They help to remove weak and diseased animals and keep everything in balance.

All skates lay egg cases, but all rays and many species of shark give birth to live babies called pups. Sharks, skates and rays don't have as many babies as other fish and their pups grow slowly, so their numbers can be easily reduced by fishing and other threats.

Beware of the Humans!

On average fewer than 10 people in the world lose their lives to shark attacks each year. Humans kill about 100 million sharks each year.

Q Fact File: Top Predators × +

Jump for Joy?

Despite the fact that they weigh several tonnes, basking sharks have been seen jumping out of the water. Nobody knows exactly why they do these enormous belly flops, although some scientists think they could be showing off to potential mates.

Speedy Swimsuits

Shark skin feels rough to touch. It has a special structure which helps a shark glide through the water easily. This idea is now being used to make boats that don't need so much fuel, and swimsuits that help athletes swim faster.

Not to be Sniffed at!

Sharks can sniff out their prey or other sharks from a great distance. Up to two thirds of the weight of a shark's brain is used for smelling things.

The Uncommon Skate

The common skate can grow to almost 3 metres long and used to be common in British waters. Due to overfishing, it is now critically endangered.

Seashore Survival Quiz

Survival is a challenge for marine wildlife.
Try out these questions and test your friends.

1 How long have sea anemones been known to live?

☐ a) 5–10 years

☐ b) 20–30 years

☐ c) 60–80 years

☐ d) 100–150 years

2 Why are sea cucumbers good for the marine environment?

☐ a) They clean the sand by pooing

☐ b) They encourage animals to eat their salad

☐ c) Litter sticks to their spines

☐ d) They eat jellyfish

3 What Indo-Pacific animal is known to pretend to be a lionfish, sea snake or a jellyfish to deter predators?

☐ a) The trickster toadfish

☐ b) The camouflage crab

☐ c) The mimic octopus

☐ d) The disguising dogfish

4 What do small-spotted catsharks do when they feel threatened?

a) Bite

b) Curl up like a doughnut and hope the threat goes away

c) Thrash their tails and splash water

d) Growl like a dog

5 Female 15-spined sticklebacks die after laying their eggs. What happens to the eggs?

a) The male makes a nest for the eggs and guards them

b) The eggs stick to grains of sand and are perfectly camouflaged

c) They are eaten by crabs but survive

d) They give off acid so nothing can eat them

How did you do?
Turn upside down to find the answers.

Answers: 1: c - 60–80 years is the longest recorded. 2: a - Many sea cucumbers hoover up sand and filter out algae that might be harmful to other marine life. 3: c - Octopus are known for their ability to change colour. 4: b - Catsharks are pussycats compared with some other sharks. They prefer to hide away. 5: a - The male secretes a special sticky substance from his kidneys to hold the seaweed together and keep the eggs safe.

CHAPTER 4

BE A WILDLIFE CHAMPION

You have already discovered how sea creatures fight for survival. Unfortunately, humans are creating environmental problems that can make this fight even harder.

Your next challenge is to explore some of the threats facing sea creatures, including litter, climate change and overfishing.

The good news is that being a **real-life superhero** and standing up for nature is easier than it sounds. There are lots of simple actions you can take. You won't need to wear a shiny cape or put your pants on over your trousers to protect your beach (unless you want to).

Balloon in a Bottle

ACTIVITY 37

Bopping balloons about is fun, but if they blow away they can land in the ocean. Find out why **marine conservationists** are worried about balloon litter with this simple experiment.

You will need a jar or pot with a watertight lid and an uninflated balloon.

- Take a walk along the tide line of your beach. You may find an old balloon, but if not use one from home. Fill your jar with seawater, put the balloon in and close the lid.

- Take a photo of the balloon.

- What do you think it will look like in a day, a week, a month or a year?

- Take a new photo of your balloon jar at the end of each week. Compare the photos after a month.

- How long does it take your balloon to break down?

What's Happening?

Balloons are made of plastic or latex (rubber) mixed with other chemicals. They can take many years to break down. Even 'biodegradable' balloons only break down properly in warm composters. They are deadly to seabirds if swallowed.

Junk Jigsaw

Plastics are useful because they can be **shaped** in many different ways. They are in our food packaging, clothes, cars and furniture and they are used to make fishing nets, buckets and spades. Plastic might seem fantastic, but it **doesn't belong** on your beach. Will you find it there?

- Explore the tide line and other areas where litter can collect such as dunes and between rocks.

- Collect the plastic you find in a bucket. Wear gloves or use a litter-picker tool to avoid touching litter.

- Organise your finds by size from largest to smallest. Are broken pieces of plastic smooth or jagged? Take care with any sharp pieces.

- Use your plastic pieces to create some beach art. You could spell out words or make a sea creature.

- Take a photo then collect up your finds and take them to a bin.

- Remember to wash your hands after touching rubbish.

Dig Deeper

How many different types of plastic can you find at home? Find out which ones can be recycled locally.

Q Fact File: Beach Litter × +

Plastics are not the only type of **litter** on the beach, but they are a problem because they stay around for a long time. **Turtles** can mistake plastic bags for the **jellyfish** they like to eat. Other **air-breathing** marine animals, like **seals** and **seabirds**, can become tangled in plastics and drown. When the sea breaks plastic into smaller pieces, marine wildlife can mistake it for plankton and eat it. This can make animals ill or even kill them.

Reducing how much plastic we use can make a difference. **Think about changes** that you can make and challenge your friends and family to do the same.

Plastic Not Your Bag?

On average, plastic bags are used for 15 minutes before they are thrown away. Always take re-usable bags to the shops!

Q Fact File: Beach Litter ✕ +

Take Back the Beaches

In 2019, volunteers cleared nearly 11 tonnes of rubbish in just one weekend as part of a national event. Plastics were the most common items removed.

Famous Namesake

A grey seal injured by a plastic frisbee around its neck was named Sir David, after Sir David Attenborough, the wildlife presenter who has campaigned to raise awareness of marine plastics.

Deep Sea Plastic

In 2014, a new species of sand hopper-like crustacean was discovered six kilometres beneath the ocean surface in the Mariana Trench. It was named *Eurythenes plasticus* after the plastic found in its stomach.

Worrying for Wildlife

Around 8 million pieces of plastic enter the world's oceans every day, adding up to 8 million tonnes per year. Plastic kills about 1 million seabirds and 100,000 marine mammals and turtles every year.

Sourcing the Source

Find out how pollution from the land gets to the sea with this exploration.

Most beaches have a stream, river or estuary flowing across them or nearby.

- Take a walk inland along the stream or river, taking care to keep to public roads and footpaths.

- Do the banks of your river look natural and healthy? Is the water clean?

- Does your river flow close to any roads, houses, businesses or farms?

- Look at the landscape around your river. The rain from the higher land around the sides of the river valley (the **river basin**) will flow into your river.

- Look at a map to find out how far the water has travelled from its **source**.

What's Happening?

When rain flows into rivers, it picks up leaves, soil and anything else it encounters along the way. This can include oil spilled on roads, animal waste, sewage, rubbish and chemicals. All rivers eventually flow into the sea, so water pollution is a problem for marine life.

Litter Investigation

Plastics and other litter on beaches are a
problem, but where does all that waste
come from?

Remember to take care when handling litter. Use **gloves** and a
litter picker if possible. Avoid sharp or dangerous objects and
wash your hands afterwards.

Go litter picking along your beach.

- Note or place each item in one of these categories:

    - Fishing waste (nets, lines, hooks, fish crates, crab
    pots, gloves, etc.)

    - Dropped on the beach (food packets, crab nets,
    drink bottles, beach shoes, plastic bags)

    - Nurdles (tiny plastic pellets which are used in
    making plastic items)

    - Polystyrene (a light, white plastic used in packaging
    that easily breaks down into squidgy balls)

    - Other (anything else that turns up)

- What are the most and least common types of litter?
Where do they come from? Has anything come from
another country?

Conservationists use information like this to better understand
how litter is moved by ocean winds and currents.

Q Fact File: Sources of Pollution × +

Plastics, stray nets, water pollution and oil spills all pose serious dangers to marine life. Better controls on river water quality and dumping waste at sea have helped to reduce some types of pollution, but there is still more to be done.

80% of the plastic in our oceans comes from the land and has been blown or washed into the sea, sometimes from hundreds of kilometres inland. Reducing our personal waste and only flushing pee, poo and paper down the toilet is the best way to stop this happening. Once litter is in the sea, it can travel huge distances. Some items float in the sea for so long that they become covered in barnacles.

Ghost Nets

640,000 tonnes of fishing nets are dumped into the world's seas each year. Turtles, whales and other marine creatures become entangled and often die.

Fact File: Sources of Pollution

Plastic Sand

Tiny pellets of plastic called nurdles are used in making plastic products. They contain harmful chemicals and are often mistaken for food by sea creatures. Nurdles are hard to remove from beaches because they mix with the sand. 53 billion nurdles are estimated to enter UK seas each year.

Beachcombing for Lego

A shipping container holding nearly 5 million pieces of Lego sank 30 kilometres from the Cornish coast in 1997. To this day, people are still finding Lego pieces on Cornwall's beaches!

Beach Bombshell!

Sunken treasure, planes, shipwrecks, crisp packets from 50 years ago, and even unexploded bombs from the Second World War have all been found on British beaches. If you see anything suspicious, stay well away and phone the Coastguard!

Investigate Why Sea Levels Are Rising

Over two-thirds of the world's surface is covered by oceans. Investigate why sea levels are rising with this simple pebble game.

- Fill a bucket nearly full of seawater and collect a pile of small pebbles.

- Guess how many you will be able to add before the bucket overflows. Challenge your family and friends to play. Take turns adding a pebble, trying not to make the bucket overflow.

What's Happening?

When something sinks in water, it moves the same volume of water as itself out of the way. This is called **displacement** and it makes the water level rise. Adding water instead of pebbles has the same effect. **Ice shelves** and **glaciers** on land are melting due to **climate change**. Meltwater and ice flow into the sea making the sea level rise.

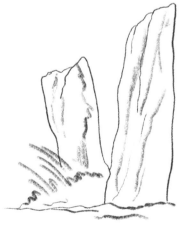

Floating ice displaces its **own weight** in water. When **sea ice and icebergs** melt, the **sea level remains the same** because the melted water weighs the same as the ice. Test this by watching ice cubes melting in a glass of water.

Plan a Climate-Friendly Beach Trip

Human activities are speeding up the **warming** of our planet's **climate**, causing problems including sea level rise. We need to reduce the amount of **fossil fuels** we use in things like driving cars and making electricity. Cutting down on what we **buy** means we reduce **greenhouse gases** and **waste**.

What would your perfect climate-friendly beach trip look like? Use these suggestions to help you plan:

- Transport: Walking or cycling are ideal. Taking a train or bus is better than using a car.

- Food: Think about using locally produced foods rather than food that has travelled from far away.

- Drink: Fill a re-usable bottle at home. Look out for re-fill water stations near your beach.

- Beach gear: Re-use old buckets and spades instead of buying new ones. Take an old food tub to catch crabs instead of using a net. Some beaches have sharing points where people can leave their used beach kit for others to borrow.

- Waste: Could you choose an ice cream cone over a tub or use re-usable bags in shops?

Q Fact File: Climate Change × +

Our planet's warmth comes from the sun's powerful rays. We'd sizzle like sausages by day and freeze like lollies at night if it wasn't for our atmosphere, which is wrapped around the Earth like a blanket, trapping some of the sun's heat. **Atmospheric gases** like carbon dioxide and methane hold the heat in. They are known as greenhouse gases and if they increase, our climate becomes hotter.

People burn coal, oil and gas to power our cars, homes and factories. These fuels come from fossils that take millions of years to form. Burning fossil fuels releases **greenhouse gases**, warming the Earth's climate, changing rainfall patterns and raising sea levels. Climate change is dangerous for humans and wildlife.

Try To Be Below Average!

In 2016, the average person in the UK produced around 8.5 tonnes of carbon dioxide per year. Reducing greenhouse gases is good in lots of ways, such as making the air cleaner, improving our diets and providing more **wild spaces** for play and nature.

Fact File: Climate Change

Underwater Mammoths!

During the last Ice Age, sea levels around the British Isles were around 120 metres lower than today. There was dry land between the UK and the Netherlands and mammoths, elk and sabre-toothed cats roamed free. Their fossilised skeletons have been found under the North Sea.

Hot Summers?

The five warmest years in UK recorded history have all taken place since 2006. This may seem like good news for beach lovers, but storms are predicted to become more frequent and a quarter of the UK's sandy coast could be lost to sea levels rising.

Worldwide Protests by Children

Swedish schoolgirl Greta Thunberg became famous after launching school strikes to protest against climate change and demand action. Millions of children around the world joined the strikes. Her book, *No One Is Too Small to Make a Difference*, became a worldwide best seller.

Make a Splash!

ACTIVITY 43

Carbon dioxide can make a **change** to the acidity of seawater that is bad for marine wildlife. Discover how it gets there with this activity, which is perfect for a sunny day.

- Stand in some shallow seawater (staying away from big waves and strong currents).

- Use your hands and feet to splash the water.

- Watch what happens to the water. Can you make bubbles?

What's Happening?

When you splash the seawater, it fills with tiny bubbles that may turn it almost white. These are air bubbles that are mixing into the water. On the surface of our oceans, the wind and waves mix air into the water.

Air contains very small amounts of **carbon dioxide,** which can dissolve in seawater. Some carbon dioxide is taken up by tiny plants called **phytoplankton,** but the rest reacts with the seawater and changes its chemistry.

Seashells in Vinegar Experiment

Increases in carbon dioxide in seawater cause **ocean acidification**. So, what does that mean and why does it matter? In this experiment you will investigate **acids**.

- Collect a small, empty sea snail shell from the beach and take it home.

- Half fill a transparent pot or jar with vinegar.

- Add your seashell. What can you see?
  (Hold it up to the light for the best view.)

- After an hour, remove your shell using a spoon. Does it look different?

- Return the shell to the vinegar and leave it overnight.

- How has the shell changed? What happens if you leave it longer?

What's Happening?

Sea snails build their shells using **calcium carbonate**. This substance is easily damaged by strong acids like vinegar. When you put the shell in vinegar it causes a chemical reaction. The shell seems to fizz because it is releasing little bubbles of carbon dioxide.

Seawater is not an acid, but its acidity is changing in ways that affect sea snails.

Q Fact File: Ocean Acidity ✕ +

When **carbon dioxide** is absorbed by the sea, it dissolves. It causes chemical changes to the water, making it slightly more acidic. The world's oceans absorbed around *2.6 billion tonnes* of carbon dioxide in 2017 and people are still putting more carbon dioxide into the atmosphere by burning fossil fuels. So, what does this mean for wildlife?

The small change in ocean acidity isn't enough to dissolve seashells but it does make it harder for snails to build their shells. Other sea creatures that build calcium carbonate structures, like corals, crabs, urchins and plankton, may also be affected. These animals are all essential to the marine food chain.

We can help protect the future of our sea creatures by not burning fossil fuels, which will reduce the carbon dioxide in our oceans.

Q Fact File: Ocean Acidity ✕ ＋

Carbon Sink

Plants and natural environments that store carbon are known as carbon sinks. Since humans began burning more fossil fuels, the seas have absorbed around 517 billion tonnes of carbon dioxide. This is great for reducing greenhouse gases, but not so great for our marine wildlife.

Not Clowning About

Lots of living things need acidity to be about the same all the time. Clownfish don't hear danger signals well and struggle to find their way home when their environment is more acidic.

Bad News for Coral Reefs

Although acidity may not directly harm all corals, scientists are worried that coral eggs seem to find it harder to settle and grow successfully in more acid conditions.

Erupting Evidence

Volcanic vents under the sea release large amounts of carbon dioxide and can make the seawater around them more acidic. Scientists are using these places to help them understand the effects of ocean acidification.

Prawn-Catching Challenge

There are lots of ways to harvest food from the oceans, but are there plenty more fish in the sea? Catch a prawn and **find out about fishing**.

common prawn

- Look for prawns in warm, shallow pools. They are well camouflaged!

- Try to catch a prawn with your hands. Watch how it moves and where it goes.

- How many can you catch in ten minutes? (Be sure to handle prawns gently, keep them in seawater and return them afterwards.)

- How might people catch lots of prawns?

- What problems might this cause?

What's Happening?

Unsurprisingly, sea creatures don't like to be caught! Prawns, flatfish and shellfish, hide away on the seabed. People have solved this problem by pulling weighted **nets** along the sea floor, catching everything in their path. This method is called **trawling** and can harm wildlife. **Farmed prawns or fish** can also be a problem because of the cramped conditions they live in, the waste in their water, and the need to catch more wild seafood to feed the farmed animals.

Use a Good Fish Guide

ACTIVITY 46

Everyone can help to protect the marine environment by making good choices.
Shops and restaurants can make a difference by buying **sustainably caught** fish and giving **information** to their customers. Discover more with this activity.

- With an adult's permission, look on the internet for a good fish guide for your area.

- Explore the guide. There will be a sustainability rating for each species and information about the different ways of fishing for it.

- Visit a local shop or look at a restaurant menu. How does the seafood rate on your guide? Is it easy to find information? How much variety is available?

- If you don't eat fish, find out about edible seaweeds and ways of harvesting them. Do your local shops and cafés sell seaweed products? Can you tell where they are from?

Dig Deeper

- Ask business owners how easy it is to buy sustainable fish. Are their customers interested in sustainability?

- Survey your family or class. What seafood do they eat? Would they try eating different species?

Q Fact File: Sustainable Seafood × +

When we harvest **food** from the sea, we need to keep a **healthy balance** by only using what can easily be replaced. If you eat fish, you can try a variety of different seafoods and make sure they are caught using methods that don't harm the environment. Support small, sustainable fishing businesses by eating locally caught seafood. Can you encourage your friends, families, schools and clubs to eat only sustainable seafoods?

Don't Throw Your Food!

Fishing boats are given permits to catch particular types of seafood. Trawling for small animals like scampi can catch lots of unwanted fish. Thousands of tonnes of fish on boats are thrown away despite this being against the law.

One for the Pot?

Edible crabs can weigh up to 4 kilograms (about the same as a cat). They can be caught in specially designed pots, from which they cannot escape. Any crabs which are too small to eat or have eggs can be safely returned to the sea.

Q Fact File: Sustainable Seafood ✕ +

Turtle Triumph

In the USA many turtles used to become trapped in shrimp trawling nets. Conservationists and fishermen worked together to introduce escape hatches into nets. Turtle strandings have since reduced by 44%.

Going Bananas to Save Dolphins?

In the UK, fishermen and conservationists have been trying out yellow devices that hook onto nets. These 'banana pingers' send out a warning sound to try to stop dolphins and porpoises from coming near.

Jellyfish and Chips

Over 90% of the cod eaten in the UK has to be imported. Meanwhile, three-quarters of the seafood caught in the UK is sold overseas because Brits won't eat it. We may need to become more adventurous to eat sustainably.

Leave a Message in the Sand

Do you think your beach is amazing? Would you like people to look after it better? This is your chance to get the **message** across.

- Decide what you would like to tell the world about. Perhaps you want to share a fact about your favourite sea creature, or to let people know how many pieces of plastic you've found?

- When you have chosen your message, write, draw or make it. You might use a stick or your foot to draw in the sand, create it with different coloured pebbles or build it from items you find on the beach.

- When you are happy with your creation, take a photo to show your friends and family.

Dig Deeper

- Can you make your message so big that it can be seen from far away?

- How about sharing your message with a group or your class to inspire others to help you look after our seas?

Make a Pledge

Thinking about the problems facing our seas can feel worrying, but small changes can make a real difference, especially if everyone joins in.

Select a pledge from the suggestions below or make up your own.

I pledge to help my beach and make the world a better place by...

☐ Buying fewer things wrapped in plastic

☐ Making sure everyone in my household recycles

☐ Only eating sustainably caught fish

☐ Eating locally grown food or growing my own

☐ Learning everything about my favourite sea creature and sharing what I know

☐ Not leaving the tap running while I brush my teeth

☐ Using less electricity

☐ Getting my family walking and cycling more instead of driving

☐ Making a poster, story, dance, song, poem or film about marine creatures and how to look after them

☐ Making new things from items that would normally be thrown away

Have fun with your pledge and see where it takes you!

Q Fact File: Make a Difference × +

Whether it's picking up litter, reducing your use of fossil fuels or sharing your love of sea creatures, there are endless ways in which every one of us can make a difference.

Be **inspired** by the successes of these incredible people and projects.

Kids Against Plastic!

When Amy and Ella Meek from Nottingham learned about the impacts of plastics, they decided to set up Kids Against Plastic. They have picked up over 60 thousand pieces of litter, done a TedX talk, built a team of children around the UK and recruited schools and organisations to their Plastic Clever scheme.

Q Fact File: Make a Difference

Crisp Campaign

Marine biology graduate Emily Stevenson from Cornwall made her graduation dress entirely out of discarded crisp packets! She wanted a crisp-making company to stop their packets from ending up on our beaches. The company now allows people to send their packets back for recycling.

Dive into Nature

At just 14 years old, Cruz Erdmann from New Zealand won the 2019 BBC Young Wildlife Photographer of the Year competition. The stunning photo that won was of a bigfin reef squid.

Seeing is Believing

Over 14 million people tuned in to *Blue Planet 2* to see the incredible footage of marine life presented by Sir David Attenborough in 2017. Awareness of climate change and ocean plastics soared and 88% of viewers said they changed their behaviour.

Wildlife Champion Quiz

Do you have what it takes to be an eco-hero? Test your knowledge with this fun quiz. Challenge your friends and family to have a go too.

1 You come across a seabird covered in oil. Should you…

- a) Help it back to the sea
- b) Try to clean it
- c) Put it in a box with air holes and call a rescue centre
- d) Give it a fish

2 Your friend steps on a weever fish and howls with pain. Do you…

- a) Try to catch the fish
- b) Pee on your friend's foot to cure it
- c) Rub it better
- d) Ask a lifeguard for hot water to bathe the foot

3 You have been invited to talk about your beach at a conference. How will you get there?

- a) Private jet (it's good to arrive in style)
- b) Convince the organiser to do a video conference instead
- c) Take a train and a taxi
- d) Ask a family member to drive me

4 You see a seal lying on a beach with a piece of fishing net around its neck. Do you…

☐ a) Take a photo and call a marine rescue group

☐ b) Go closer to take a clearer photo

☐ c) Try to catch the seal and cut through the net

☐ d) Leave it alone – the net will fall off eventually

5 What marine wildlife is likely to suffer from the negative effects of ocean acidification?

☐ a) Pteropods and foraminifera (zooplankton)

☐ b) Corals

☐ c) Fish

☐ d) All of the above

How did you do?
Turn upside down to find the answers.

Answers: 1: c – Oiled birds need urgent specialist help from a rescue centre. 2: d – It's a myth that you should wee on jellyfish or weever fish stings! Hot water breaks down the venom. 3: b – Taking public transport is good, but walking, cycling or not travelling at all is even better. 4: a – Seals can get hurt if they are disturbed. If you see a marine mammal in difficulty, call a marine rescue group. 5: d – Ocean acidification could affect the whole marine food chain.

CONGRATULATIONS!

YOU'RE A BEACH EXPLORER

Amazing work! You have discovered how your beach was made, what it is like to live there and equipped yourself to be a marine conservation champion by investigating the challenges your beach faces.

The fun doesn't stop here. Take on these two last activities and you could be set up for a lifetime of wonder.

Join a Group

By sharing our love of nature and tackling problems
together, we can make a huge difference. Whether
you would like to become an expert on dolphins or run
a campaign to stop marine pollution, there is a group out there
that would love to have you on board.

- Take part in activities run by volunteer groups at your beach
  and ask how to get involved.

- Look up marine conservation charities and contact them.
  They'll tell you how you can take part in their wildlife recording
  programmes, beach cleans and other projects.

- If you can't find a group or organisation to match your
  interests, why not start your own?

Adopt a Beach

After completing the activities in this book, you know your
beach better than anyone. So, why not adopt your beach
and look after it for life?

- Visit regularly and record the wildlife you see on iSpot Nature
  or with your Wildlife Trust.

- Do a beach clean every time you visit, or organise one each
  month and invite friends and family to help you.

- Keep a written, photo or video diary about your beach. What
  changes do you see? How does your beach make you feel?

- Tell others about your beach. If you can persuade others to
  share your passion, they will help you to look after it.

Wacky Marine Wildlife Names

Every known species of living thing has a scientific name. It is usually made of two words. *Patella vulgata* is the scientific name for the common limpet. The first word is like a surname, telling you what group the species belongs to, and the second word is the unique name of the species.

Scientific names are essential for biologists but can be a bit of a mouthful, so people often use common names based on what they think the animal or plant looks like. Check out these fabulous names…

Don't Try Eating These!

Shredded carrot and mashed potato sponges look just like their names! Other sea creatures that look like foods are baked bean sea squirts and strawberry anemones.

Halloween Party Guests?

Spooky marine creature names include dead man's fingers (a soft coral), goosebump sponges, devil's tongue seaweed and lumpsucker fish

Underwater Zoo

Some sea creatures look like other animals. Look out for goose barnacles, elephant hide sponge and the sea mouse (a hairy worm)!

Look all of these creatures up and see for yourself!

Did you know that a baby puffin is called a puffling? What other bizarre names can you discover? Have fun inventing your own names for the animals and seaweeds you find.

BEFORE YOU GO...

There are some things we just can't help doing, like breathing, blinking and exploring beaches. My own fascination began with picking up bright seashells as a tiny toddler and it never stopped. Whether I'm writing, taking groups out on the beach or campaigning for our wildlife, I am always amazed by nature and by all the wonderful people who work together to look after our marine environment.

Whatever grabs your interest, I hope that the activities in this book will set you on your own path of discovery. Keep exploring, keep having fun, keep standing up for wildlife and who knows where it might lead you?

What Next?

There are lots of fabulous resources available to help you find out all about beaches, wildlife and conservation. Here are a few to get you started.

Books

Kids Fight Plastic, Martin Dorey
Benny the Blenny's Shallow Sea Adventure, Teresa Naylor
Seashore Safaris, Judith Oakley
RSPB Handbook of the Seashore, Maya Plass
The Essential Guide to Rockpooling, Steve Trewhella and Julie Hatcher
The Essential Guide to the Strandline, Steve Trewhella and Julie Hatcher

Organisations and Websites

Accessible Countryside
for Everyone (ACE)   http://www.accessiblecountryside.org.uk/
Friends of the Earth   https://friendsoftheearth.uk/
Keep Britain Tidy   https://www.keepbritaintidy.org/
Kids Against Plastic   https://www.kidsagainstplastic.co.uk/
Marine Biological Association   https://www.mba.ac.uk/
Marine Conservation Society   https://www.mcsuk.org/
National Trust   https://www.nationaltrust.org.uk/
National Trust for Scotland   https://www.nts.org.uk/
Natural History Museum
(Seaweed and Fossil apps)   https://www.nhm.ac.uk/take-part.html
iSpot   https://www.ispotnature.org/
Irish Whale and Dolphin Group   https://iwdg.ie/
Irish Wildlife Trust   https://iwt.ie/
Rockwatch   https://www.rockwatch.org.uk/
Royal Society for the Protection
of Birds (RSPB)   https://www.rspb.org.uk/
Surfers Against Sewage   https://www.sas.org.uk/
The Shark Trust   https://www.sharktrust.org/
Whale and Dolphin Conservation   https://uk.whales.org/
Wildlife Trusts   https://www.wildlifetrusts.org/

Index

If you loved this book, you might enjoy these...

ISBN 978-1912836253

ISBN 978-1912836284